THE
LAST
PRAYER

MICHAEL E. GOINGS

The Last Prayer
Copyright © 2024 by Michael E. Goings

TABLE OF CONTENTS

CHAPTER 1

THE LAST PRAYER

It was one fine day. The sky was blue, the sun had some heat in it, and the breeze was cool and easy. The surroundings were filled with the usual noise–children on the playground, the couples on the park, the animals of all kinds chasing each other, the vendors on the streets, and the song on the radio. Everything was pretty much the same, as Luke would say. Everyday was the same, as he would say. Luke drove past the park and towards his destination.

When Luke arrived at the Department of Motor Vehicles for some business, a sign about being an organ donor caught his attention. Luke had already given it a thought before.

"It would be nice to donate my organs once I die," He thought once.

Be it due to natural causes or an accident, donating his organs after his death will continue to prove his truth to his values and morals. Seeing the sign, Luke felt compelled in his heart to donate. He remembers how another person's blood had saved his mother's life after she lost too many while giving birth to him. Luke's parents, both devout Christians, had constantly told him that God had some great purpose for him. They told him that it was one of the very many reasons why both he and his mother were spared through the blood of someone else.

His father–a pastor who loves to preach and teach by taking natural illustrations and comparing them with the scriptures–compared the blood that had been donated to save Luke and his mother's lives to the blood of

Jesus. He compares it to the blood of Jesus; the blood being shed to save sinners from their sin and living in hell eternally. Luke's father compared this random person's blood to the blood of Jesus.

So, now that Luke was an adult and a Christian himself, with a wife and two children, the words that his parents had repeatedly told him would constantly resound in his mind.

"You have a special purpose in life, given to you by God," They constantly reminded him. Then, they ran on to talk about the blood of another being the entire reason for his life being spared. Every chance they get, they tell Luke how it was because of that person's benevolent act that he lives. And Luke did not forget. Luke was a faithful member in his church. He endeavored to be both a good husband to his wife and a good father to his children. Luke would reckon he was a good citizen to his community as well.

All these things he could consider as something that a good Christian could live. All these things that he could name as 'payment' for given life; living a good life in accordance to what God would love. All these and Luke still did not understand what was the special purpose God had spared him for.

He had not felt the call to the ministry as his father had at an early age. Some people, perhaps well-meaning people, had always convinced him that his calling was going to be the same as his father's. After all, he was his father's son and a preacher's kid. This was especially the case for some who had knowledge of their circumstances at his birth. However, such prophecies, desires, or wishes from others seem to never agree with what he felt in his heart. Luke was never the kind to claim a calling or a gift that he had not been fully convinced that the Lord had given him. No, he didn't doubt the words his parents had told him about his purpose and about the story surrounding his birth. He believed it. Only that, he would just want to continue to wait on that "calling" until the day the Lord revealed it to him.

He had already signed the papers as he overcame the reluctance to become an organ donor. Luke had taken the necessary steps so that his wishes would be carried out by the time anything untoward ever happens to him. After he signed the papers and had done his business with the Department of Motor Vehicles, he drove home.

When he got home, he shared the news with his wife and children. They all discussed it over dinner. They had their reservations regarding it, like some cultural superstitions.

They said, "Most people died shortly after they signed up to become an organ donor."

Luke humored them. He assured his family that his life was solely in the hands of God.

"God has a purpose with me and I honestly believe I won't die until I have fulfilled that purpose," He asserted with confidence, "Before I signed up to be an organ donor, I prayed that when I do die, He will let anyone who receives any of my blood or organs be a sinner who needed saving. And if it was His Will, to bring them to a saving knowledge of Jesus Christ". These words had satisfied and calmed the apprehension in his family and assured them that everything was completely in the Sovereign Hands of God.

The night had ended and Luke seemed pretty pleased with himself. He carried on with his life. He continued being a man of conviction and integrity, especially in regards to his walk with the Lord.

Luke was pretty much known for his faithfulness in the church, so he had a good reputation in their community. This was the primary reason why their pastor had met with him in a private meeting. He wanted him to give some serious thought about becoming either a Deacon or Trustee of the church. Luke did not decline nor accept to be appointed and ordained to either position. He was serious about anything pertaining to the things of God and, especially, the position of leadership on any level and, unlike some; he was not motivated by personal ambition and eagerness to obtain a position in the church.

"I will consider it, Pastor. I would immediately call you once I am convinced that my decision is indeed a calling from the Lord," He assured his pastor. The pastor gave him a warm smile.

"You're a good man, Luke. I'm sure the Lord will want you to be one of his servants," The pastor tapped him on the shoulder. He no longer had the urge to coerce or pressure him since he felt Luke's sincerity through his words.

In the ensuing days after his meeting with his pastor, one of the things that stayed on his mind was the words from his parents that he had heard nearly his entire life.

"Son, the Lord spared you because he has a special purpose for your life."

He was 30 years old. Up to this age, he still does not know what exactly that purpose was. He knew, like all believers, that he was called to worship God. He was being called to be a witness for Him, through character and behavior. He was called to act upon it as a good father, a good husband, and good citizen. And all these things, he had done it religiously. He had even decided–finally–to become an organ donor after grappling with the idea for years now.

He was 30 years old and he still did not know his purpose.

But he was already close to knowing that purpose.

One dark morning, something happened suddenly that would bring unexpected grief and sadness to his family, friends, relatives, and those who knew him dearly.

Luke was on his way to work one morning. It was still dark and extremely foggy. A pickup truck swerved into his lane and caused a head-on collision. The man driving the truck survived with some minor injuries. However, Luke was killed on contact.

CHAPTER 2

FROM REBELLION TO REDEMPTION

It began raining. Luke's car was head on with the truck it had a collision with and the smoke coming from each car was filling in their surroundings. The other man was unconscious, with scratches and bleeding on the head. Luke, however, was unresponsive. The people on the side of the road, who had witnessed the collision, immediately dialed 911.

When the emergency medical team arrived, along with a few law enforcement officers, they saw the bracelet on Luke's right wrist. It was the bracelet that certifies he was an organ donor. The response team notified his family and arrangements were made to send his body to a hospital where he could be honored as an organ donor. Immediately after the blood and organs were taken from the corpse of Luke, they were put in a place to preserve them from any decay or deterioration.

Luke's family was devastated. Everyone who Luke dearly love was devastated. They sat around together after his burial, in silence because for once, they do not know which words to say. Their silence was momentarily broken off by sniffles and sighs. His family were in constant tears, as they remember what the head of their family prayed for before his untimely death.

"God has a purpose with me and I honestly believe I won't die until I have fulfilled that purpose. Before I signed up to be an organ donor, I prayed that when I do die, He will let anyone who receives any of my blood or organs be a sinner who needed saving. And if it was His Will, to bring them to a saving knowledge of Jesus Christ."

They waited for the call from a hospital or a medical facility, saying that someone was finally a match to receive one of his organs or his bloods. Suddenly, there was an event, unknowingly unfolding beneath their teary eyes.

Unbeknownst to anyone, but the Lord, a young man named Edward Fuller had been part of a gang who were known for drug trafficking, violence, and even murder. Edward was raised by his grandmother, who was a Christian woman. She had brought him up, attending church each Sunday. He had, regrettably, been an environmental or cultural Christian and had never truly accepted Christ into his heart as his Lord and Savior.

Edward's grandmother passed away about a year ago and since then, he had been lured into the streets. He had completely forsaken the teachings of his dear grandmother and what he had learned from his Sunday school teacher and youth pastor. Edward had some anger and resentment in him, both towards God and the church, whom he blindly blamed for the passing of the most endearingly precious person in his life.

Edward Fuller was in his most vulnerable state. This also meant being vulnerable to the tactics that the gang used to attract new members. Edward had to go through an initiation and pass a test in order to be part of them. He was tasked to be a part of the hit squad that was assigned to assassinate a member of a rival gang as a requirement. After fulfilling this, he was now a bona fide member with a kill to his name. This was of great importance in the warped estimation of other gang members. However, this distinction of membership came with a great price. Edward was now a marked man. He was now on the hit list by the gang whose member he had helped to kill.

The day came when the seed that he had sown through violence, drug dealing, and murder would come knocking at his door. Unbeknownst to him, as he and one of his gang buddies were cruising in his car and stopped at a traffic light, a car belonging to the rival gang pulled up beside them. Before he and his buddy could pull out of harm's way, a volley of bullets from semi-automatic firearms came through the passenger side killing Edward's buddy immediately and seriously wounding him in the process.

He was rushed to the hospital by the emergency personnel. One of the bullets had severed an artery in his torso on the right side. Although the paramedics worked intensely to stop Edward from losing more blood en route to the closest hospital, he went into convulsions and stopped breathing for about 10 seconds. He had lost a lot of blood and the paramedics could no longer sense any heartbeat or breathing. They looked at their watch to announce the time of his death.

"Time of death—

"No, look!"

Then, something miraculous happened right before their eyes.

"He's breathing again!" the paramedics exclaimed. Edward regained consciousness and the bleeding stopped as though the severed artery had been cauterized.

He was immediately rushed into surgery as soon as they arrived at the hospital. The surgeon and his team wasted no time and their attempt to locate where the bleeding was coming from. Though it had stopped for some mysterious, or perhaps miraculous, reason, if they were to save his life, it was essential that they locate where the bleeding was stemming from. When they finally located the artery that had been severed, they were completely astounded at what they discovered.

The blood from the severed artery had coagulated into a solidified mask. This congealing was enough to stop Edward from dying from a loss of blood. Everyone who worked with the surgical team was mystified at what they saw. All of them sat there in confusion as to how it could have possibly happened. Some immediately knew there was a "higher power" that definitely intervened in Edward's seemly, certain demise.

"Someone up there must really love this young man," a staff member stated.

The surgeon and his team carried on the operation despite their bewilderment. Once they repaired the severed artery, they gave him some blood plasma to replace the massive amount of blood he had lost.

It took days for Edward to come off the ventilator and from being sustained intravenously. However, when he was drifting in and out of consciousness, he would often hear the voice of his grandmother. He could hear her instructing him and pleading with him to stop his rebellious ways.

Edward could hear her telling him to accept Jesus Christ as his personal Lord and Savior.

Edward's grandmother would always tell him, when she was alive, that going to church was a good and commendable thing, but it did not mean that one was truly saved just because they attended church. He could recall the words his grandmother would always tell him.

"People can attend church without being a true Christian, but all true Christians believe in belonging to and regularly attending a Bible believing and Christ-centered church."

A few days later, Edward had gotten stronger and his vitals were all registering normal. An elderly gentleman entered Edward's room one day during his recovery. This gentleman made visiting people in hospitals and nursing homes a part of his mission in life. When he entered, he greeted Edward and asked how his day was going. Edward did not know who the old man was, but he was polite enough to greet him back anyway.

.After a few minutes of casual talk, he asked him if he was born again through believing in Jesus Christ as his Lord and Savior. Edward paused for a while before giving him an answer. He quickly recalled the words of his dear grandmother that had been cemented in his memory and said to the gentleman, "No, Sir, I am not born again." At those words, the elderly man asked him very politely, "Would you be willing to accept Jesus Christ into your heart right now?"

Edward could no longer remove the words of his grandmother. If Edward was asked this question a few days ago, he would disagree with no doubt and with full conviction. But Edward just survived a gun attack and was revived after almost dying. Suddenly, he was compelled in his heart to answer the old man. He knew he had already been convicted and prepared by the Holy Spirit. He responded to the question.

"I would." The old man led him in a simple prayer and Edward could feel he was immediately born again.

Everyone who knew of how his grandmother had brought him up in church and always prayed for him to be truly saved one day rejoiced at the good news of what had taken place. Perhaps no one knew, except the Lord, that the saving of Edward Fuller was an answer to the prayers of two people—his grandmother and a man called Luke whose blood was a factor and essential element in saving his life.

CHAPTER 3

A New Heart

Immediately after the accident, Luke's organs were removed and stored once it had been released. It was sent to a medical facility where people who can be compatible with his organs and blood can contact. It didn't even last a full day since the removal when someone called the facility, waiting for a heart. The caller said it was a man in his mid-40s who had been waiting for years already for a heart.

The name of the man was Lester Wallace. Lester was a very prominent and wealthy man, who had inherited a fortune from his father. His wealth and his prominence in the small southern town where he lived were generational. They were what some termed as "old money" and prestige. His great grandfather had founded a textile business that started small and grew exponentially over the years, due to the great demand for the fabric they produced. Lester was the 4th Wallace to take the helm of the family business once his father had suffered a stroke. The sudden demise of his father rendered him both mentally and physically unable to run the multimillion-dollar enterprise, which utterly meant that Lester found out that if he had any hopes of staying alive, he needed a new heart.

When the news came that a new heart was available and on the way, he and his family were extremely elated and relieved that a match had been made available. Regrettably, Lester was not only old school when it came to money and prominence, but he was also a sophisticated racist who had grown up in a culture and environment that firmly embraced a belief in white supremacy and segregation. He was reluctant to hire blacks at his textile plant and only did so to avoid a class action lawsuit. Even then, it was only a token few who were not given the same wages and opportunities for promotion or supervisory positions as their white counterparts. Lester was very civic minded and a member of the board of a few non-profit organizations in his locale. He was on the board of deacons at the church he had been a member of all his life. Nevertheless, though he was a regular attendee, along with his wife and children, and had even been baptized when he was a young teenager, he had truly never accepted Christ into his heart as his Lord and Savior.

There was an elderly Black woman who had been employed by the family for over 50 years as a clean-up person and babysitter when they needed her. In all actuality, she had helped to raise Lester and his younger siblings. They often referred to her as Nanny Nelly.

Nanny Nelly was a very devout Christian and had been so ever since she was a young girl. Lester and his entire family were very fond of the elderly black woman and actually regarded her as one of the family. Nanny Nelly was very bold and outspoken about her faith and would often say to Lester:

"Mr. Lester, I know you go to church about every Sunday, but you sure you truly saved?" She would ask him. Lester would snicker at this question and baffled the answer.

"Nanny, I had been baptized when I was a teenager. Of course, I am saved!" Lester would answer. His nanny was never satisfied with that answer, so she would reply invariably.

"Mr. Lester, you know I known you for a long, long time and helped your parents to raise you and your brother and your sister. I love y'all as if y'all my own. I do not want you to be lost." Nanny Nelly told him, with the utmost sincerity she had in her heart. Lester disliked the topic, he would dismiss her, avoid answering the question by either changing the subject or quickly leaving her presence by pretending that he had some urgent business to attend to. However, he could not escape the thought of her bothersome question that continued to echo within his mind.

For years, that thought never left him.

One night while he slept, he had a very disturbing and frightening dream. In the dream, he was being operated on. During the surgical procedure to replace his original heart with the new one that someone had graciously donated to him, he died. When he awakened, he was petrified by the environment where he was. It was unfamiliar. It was hot and it was uncomfortable and it was making him uneasy. It was horrible. Lester tried to look around, trying to find answers to the big question in his head.

"Where am I?" he asked.

Somehow, he was able to discern and deduce that this horrible place was what the Bible had described as hell. His senses were still intact perhaps more so than they had ever been. In utter shock, he could hear the sound of people hollering and screaming as though they were in excruciating agony and pain. The place smelled like sulfur and there was a stifling odor that burned Lester's nostrils. He heard the groaning and moaning of a multitude of people, but could not see them due to the gross darkness that permeated the entire place. Suddenly, as he grappled with the reality of his predicament, a mysterious man came to him from out of nowhere. This other worldly person spoke to Lester's mind telepathically.

"Lester Wallace. You are in the place of the damned and doomed to atone for your sins," the other worldly person spoke. Lester's forehead creased.

"What sin?" he exclaimed.

"You did not accept the One sent from God," the other worldly person replied, this time with a monstrous smile on his face.

Lester did not take a second to understand what the other worldly person was talking about. He was talking about Jesus Christ. Lester was aware and he was more aware now. He had been baptized, been brought up in church, and eventually joined the church. All of these, but he never truly accept Jesus Christ in his heart as his Lord and Savior.

He wept bitterly for his mistake and cried out to God for a second chance. His crying and pleading became so loud and intense that it awakened his wife who shook him to wake him from his dream. She inquired if he was having a nightmare. Though it was indeed a sight of a nightmare, Lester was convinced that the Lord had spoken to him in the dream.

It was Sunday morning and his heart transplant surgery was scheduled to be performed on Tuesday. Lester got up with a glitter in his eyes and a glow on his face as he prepared to go to church. His family could not avoid noticing that there was something different about him on this Sunday morning that they had never seen before. There was this very foreign aura emitting from Lester–excitement and eagerness to attend church.

The minister's sermon was thought provoking as usual and as his custom was, he made a plea to anyone who would be willing to stand and step forward to accept Jesus Christ as their Lord and Savior. There was a great hush, a sacred silence within the church as Lester rushed to the front of the spellbound congregation with all eyes fastened on him as he stood before the pastor along with a few others who were led in the sinner's prayer. When the prayer had ended and there were only a few dry eyes in the congregation, Lester asked the pastor if he could permit him to say a few words. The pastor gave him the stage.

Without any intimidation or reservation, he said, "All of these years, ever since I got baptized as a young teenager, I thought I was saved. However, it was not until last night that the Lord showed me that I was not truly born again and that if I had died, I would have landed right in hell. On Tuesday, I will be getting a new physical heart if the procedure goes well and if my Lord is willing. Today, I got a new spiritual heart and Christ truly lives within me and I am ready for whatever His will is."

Little did Lester know that the man whose heart would save his life and whose last prayer would be instrumental in him coming to accept Jesus Christ as his Lord and Savior was a Black man.

CHAPTER 4

I WAS BLIND, BUT NOW I SEE

Walter joined the Marines after the attack on the World Trade Center that took place on September 11, 2001. Watching the Twin Towers burn and crumble to the ground, due to being struck by the two jumbo passenger planes that were piloted by terrorists, Walter's heart was filled with hatred and vengeance toward the people who had done this and everyone who had any complicity to this horrible act of terrorism. A sense of patriotism and duty had compelled him to volunteer and enlist in the Marines. He chose the leathernecks because they were almost always the first to see battle.

His desire to strike back and inflict vengeance upon the people who had perpetrated the deadliest attacks on American soil since the bombing of Pearl Harbor possessed him like a demon. After basic training and advanced Individual Training, he was stationed on an aircraft carrier where he quickly disembarked with his battalion into the enemy's territory. Walter's almost insatiable desire to strike back was now being realized.

He immediately distinguished himself amongst his comrades as an outstanding Marine. Being the trigger man of a team who manned an M50 caliber machine gun, Walter meted out vengeance and death to many of his adversaries with much delight and satisfaction that fed and fueled his hatred and wrath. Walter was filling himself with so much satisfaction that he was unable to expect something tragic.

A day came when he would become a victim of his own allies' misdirected artillery shell. A shell exploded very close to where he and his team were positioned, instantly killing his buddies and blinding him in the process. When he was medevacked to a military hospital, they discovered that though he had survived the explosion, he was blind due to damage in his cornea in both of his eyes.

The loss of his sight was unknown to him because they had wrapped a bandage around his head that covered both of his eyes. The optometrist and nurses, who were assigned to his case, did everything within their power to prepare him for the worst, knowing in advance that the cornea in both of his eyes had been damaged beyond repair. When the bandages were finally removed from his eyes, Walter cried out in horror.

"I can't see! I can't see!" He was frantic.

When they were finally able to calm him, the doctor comforted and assured him that all hope of him seeing again was not lost. He explained to him, with much effort and empathy, that others had regained their ability to see who had suffered the loss of their sight by an accident or incident that damaged or destroyed their cornea in both eyes, as he had. He also told him that due to the fact that his loss of sight occurred on the battlefield in the line of duty defending his nation, his name would be at the very top as a recipient for a pair of cornea from an organ donor.

All that the doctor said to Walter was very positive and gave him something to truly hope for that one day his sight could be restored. Nevertheless, it did not extinguish the hatred that was bottled up in his heart that he had greatly kindled through the killing of many on the battlefield. He had the time from killing the enemy in defense of America to enjoying the taking of life. Now that he was blind and had become so by friendly fire, his anger and bitterness was exacerbated.

Walter became withdrawn. He became very difficult to communicate with and would occasionally display his anger and frustration out on those who had been assigned to help him through therapy and counseling. One such person was Chaplain Rogers, who was a very devout and committed Christian. He took being a chaplain very seriously. Chaplain Rogers had a secret that he kept concealed from Walter and insisted to all the others in the veteran's hospital who interacted with him to not share it with him.

He was born blind and had never been able to see. When Walter, in his deep-rooted anger and bitterness, would vent out toward others and even to Chaplain Rogers at times, he would simply ignore him. He did not react to anything that Walter would say.

"None of you all know what I am going through! You all have your sight and can see, but look at me! I am a blind man and became this way defending my country!" Walter would often exclaim. Chaplain Rogers would still hold his peace and maintain his secret. Though he was very tempted at times to share it with Walter, something down on the inside would restrain him from doing so.

As time passed, Chaplain Rogers could discern that his prayers, love, and patience were beginning to have a positive and profound effect on Walter. His attitude was changing and he had spoken less and less about the loss of his sight, as well as the hatred that he once harbored in his heart. When Chaplain Rogers would read scriptures to him and explain them, Walter would have quite a few questions to ask him. This was especially the case when it came to passages about Jesus Christ and Him being the Only Begotten Son of God who the Father sent to be the Savior of the world.

When Chaplain Rogers perceived that Walter was ready, through having heard the word and the convincing power of the Holy Spirit, he asked him if he would like to receive Jesus Christ into his heart as his Lord and Savior.

"Walter, I have something to ask you," Chaplain Rogers began, in a soft manner. Walter, sitting on the edge of his hospital bed, nodded. Chaplain Rogers heaved a sigh before proceeding.

"Are you ready to receive Jesus Christ as your Lord and Savior?" Chaplain Rogers was preparing himself with whatever response he was going to receive, but he was not baffled when he saw the younger man nod his head, much so without hesitation.

Amazingly, almost immediately thereafter, Walter received some very good news that he was to receive a pair of cornea for his eyes that could possibly restore the vision in both his eyes. He was a perfect match for the corneas from a donor who had recently died. Chaplain Rogers prayed with him with the petition that God would restore his sight, if it was His will. Walter, who was now a man with a new and converted heart, agreed.

When the procedure which lasted for a few hours was finally over, Walter was taken to a recovery room. He waited there with great expectation to have his head unwrapped from the bandages that covered his eyes. Before the surgery, he had made a special request to Chaplain Rogers to be present with him when they took the bandages from his eyes. Whatever the outcome would be, he knew he would need his moral support.

When they finally finished unwrapping the bandages, he could only see light at first. However, as he continued to blink both eyelids, his vision became clearer and clearer until it was as good as it had been before he lost his sight on the battlefield. He immediately recognized Chaplain Rogers—the man who had been used by God to get him to the place of spiritual and natural healing where he was now.

However, he was shocked to see Chaplain Rogers' stance. He was sitting in front of him, maybe a feet away, with a mobility cane in hand. He was perplexed to see that the man, whom he had sworn before that never understood about his situation, was actually the one person who understood him the best. Walter felt so much contrition and regret for the way he acted about his blindness.

"Chaplain, please forgive me. I was foolish! All I thought about was myself! All I saw was my suffering! I didn't even consider the pain of others and your pain!" Walter cried into Chaplain Rogers arms. The ever so loving old gentlemen patted Walter at the back. Chaplain Rogers told him that his blindness was not a liability, but a gift from God.

"Worry no more, child. You think you have only been blind once, but you had been blind for so long now. However, that changes today. You are no longer blind, spiritually and physically, for you can see now clearly about God and his blessings for you."

CHAPTER 5

A New Breath of Life

Beverly Baxter had been a cigarette smoker ever since she was a sophomore in high school. At first, she had been reluctant to smoke due to the fact that her grandfather, who had helped to raise her, died from lung cancer. But Beverly was a high school girl—peer pressure was common. In order to be accepted by her peers, she became a social smoker. One thing led to the other and she was already smoking a pack of cigarettes every two days by the time she was in her early 30's.

Although she never developed lung cancer, when she finally gained enough determination to kick the habit, her lungs had been seriously damaged by the many years that she had been a chain smoker.

"You will need a lung transplant," Said the doctor to Beverly.

She had herself checked when she suffered a very strong cough that has already been going on for days. Apparently, her lungs have been damaged so much by the smoking that it could no longer be cured by other forms of treatment. A lung transplant was what Beverly needed if she wanted to continue to live. Beverly did not hesitate and signed up to be put on the list of being a candidate for a new set of lungs. She had been waiting for some time now. The longer the time went by, the more desperate she became.

Beverly had been married for a few years to a man who spent a lot of time on the road as a truck driver. He was on the road more than he would be at home with her. At first, she did not take issue with the fact that he would seldom be at home. After all, he had convinced her that the reason he spent so much time on the road was because he was trying to make enough money to build her a house. That was a grand idea and she accepted it without any complaint or difficulty. However, what she discovered, almost by accident, floored her.

One day, while washing a pair of his pants, a piece of paper fell out of a pocket onto the floor. When she picked it up, out of curiosity, she read it. There were a few names of women and their phone numbers on it. Already curious, she became suspicious about the names and the numbers so much so that she was compelled to call each of them. When the voice on the other end of each call was a woman, she pretended to be his sister and told them the same lie in order to see if they would tell her the truth. Her lie was that she was calling to tell them that he had been in a serious accident.

"Oh my god, Jack! Is he alright? Which hospital is he in right now? I need to visit him! I cannot live my life without him!" Said one of the girls she called. Beverly, as she should, was enraged. She screamed on the phone, each after their reaction, and told them she was the wife. She fussed and cursed each one of them out as each immediately hung up their phone.

Beverly went up to Jack when he came home and confronted him. Of course, he denied it. He tried to deny it at first, but he utterly failed, so he shifted the blame to her.

"You didn't love me enough! So I had to find it from another woman!" He shouted. Beverly slapped him and it deafened the chaos between them. Beverly, with her shaky hands, pointed at Jack.

"You betrayed me…"

Beverly wasn't as naive as Jack thought she was. After their confrontation, she left him. She filed for a divorce and never looked back.

It had already been a few years since her divorce when Beverly heard the bad news about her lungs. Already grappling to recover emotionally and mentally, this bad news completely floored her into a state of chronic depression where she entertained suicide as an escape from her anxiety and bewilderment. Unbeknownst to Beverly, Marie, a close friend and relative, had been praying for her. Marie had been praying for her ever since the day Beverly told her about the situation she was in between her and her husband.

Marie was known to be a committed Christian and intercessor that had helped many come through their troubles by her encouraging words and prayers. When Beverly finally got around to sharing with her the bad news concerning her lungs, Marie made it a part of her daily assignment to call or come to see her in person. She was the one who had persuaded Beverly to put herself on the list to receive a set of lungs from an organ donor. At first, Beverly had been very reluctant and a bit superstitious about receiving an organ from a deceased person. She actually believed that when one got an organ from a dead person, that organ would give the spirit of the deceased the right to come and haunt them like a ghost haunts an old house. However, Marie's prayers and ability to show her in the scriptures that when people die, they do not and cannot come back, helped to dispel her superstition and convinced her to put herself on the list and receive a donor's lungs.

However, Beverly was not out of the woods yet. She continued to battle anxiety, depression, and even suicide ideation. Coupled with these evil and detrimental emotions, Beverly was harboring unforgiveness and bitterness in her heart toward her former husband for his betrayal. As she sank ever deeper into the hole that she had put herself in, Marie knew that one of Beverly's problems was stemming from her deep rooted unforgiveness and bitterness. This was second only to the fact that she had not received Jesus Christ into her heart as her Lord and Savior.

Marie had tried to avoid being pushy about the matter of her accepting Christ and used tact and patience in her effort. Nevertheless, she felt that Beverly had too much at stake for her to be too easy on her now about her salvation and eternal destiny hanging in the balance. Marie decided to add a few days of fasting, coupled with her praying, for Beverly to both accept Christ and to be successful in her waiting for a pair of lungs.

A day came when Beverly would receive sad, but honest, news from her doctors. Her breathing and condition had gotten worse and the doctors were already very concerned.

"At this rate, you'd need a miracle for a pair of lungs to become available real soon or you would die," Said the doctor. Beverly was speechless. She didn't know what to do with the information. She had been entertaining the idea of suicide for the past few months now, but the sudden thought of her condition being the one to kill her off sent shivers down her spine.

"I'm afraid you'll only live up to six month, Beverly, unless we find a donor for you."

Beverly was sunken. She did not know what to do. Her was mind was in a faze as she went back home from the hospital. Her mind was clouded with thousands and millions of thoughts, but it all came down to one thing. Marie.

When Marie went back to her friend after fasting and praying for her for a few days, she was overjoyed to find Beverly with a totally different attitude.

"Hi, Beverly. You seem so happy today," Marie commented along with her greetings toward her friend. Beverly smiled timidly.

"I want to know more about Him, Marie. I want to know more about Jesus Christ."

She possessed an eagerness to hear about Jesus Christ and how he died on the cross to save anyone from their sins who would accept him. Marie, sensing that the Holy Spirit had convicted her, immediately offered her Christ and led her in the sinner's prayer. As Beverly repeated the prayer, tears streamed from her eyes indicating her sincerity. She was now a born-again child of God, a new creation, and joint heir with Christ.

Not many days after she received Jesus Christ into her heart as her Lord and Savior, Beverly got a call from her doctor that they had found a pair of lungs for her that would be a perfect match. An organ donor had recently died and his blood type made his lungs a perfect match for Beverly. Unbeknownst to her and everyone who was connected to her struggle and eventual triumph, was a man named Luke who had made a special prayer to God that was being fulfilled. Once the transplant operation had been successfully performed and Beverly had recuperated from the surgery, she had a new breath of life in both the spiritual and natural.

CHAPTER 6

THE HOPE OF A DYING MAN

Ever since James was old enough to work, he had been a hustler. Even at the age of 12, while other boys were busy playing ball and doing other fun things, James was busy making a hustle. He would be raking leaves, mowing lawns, and doing anything that anyone in his neighborhood needed him to do. Once he became a young adult, his embrace of the work ethic did not diminish, but increased.

James became a truck driver once he was of the right age. As a truck driver, he was able to understand the mechanisms and how things could easily be transported using a truck. It wasn't long enough until he started his own trucking company after working for others. Through much diligence and sacrifice, he was able to purchase his own rig. From that initial investment, his trucking business grew to the point of him owning a fleet of 18-wheelers. James's diligence and business savvy was paying off. He was now a bona fide self-made millionaire who employed over 100 people to include drivers, mechanics, secretaries, and a full-time accountant.

Perhaps James's one glaring weakness, other than the fact that he was a self-avowed atheist, was covetousness. Over the years, he became a slave to his money ever since he started working. When he attended church, though having been forced to do so as a child, he once heard the preacher say to the congregation, "People, money is a good servant, but a poor master!" Though he never truly learned the gist of those words, James had, in actuality, made money his god. However, in spite of his greed, he was a liberal and generous man who helped quite a few people through his donations to the poor and needy, as well as some charitable nonprofit organizations.

James, in spite of being a very active and busy man that was very diligent in keeping a handle on his business, was in good physical health. He was serious about keeping his routine doctor's appointments. However one day, to his utter dismay, the last visit to his doctor had revealed some abnormality and dysfunction of his liver.

After being referred to a specialist, James was given an unfavorable and bad prognosis. For some strange reason, his liver was beginning to only function at a 40 percent capacity.

"The best, and probably your only hope, is a new liver," The specialist told him, not wanting to give him any false hope. However, James shook his head.

"Livers are very great in demand and very short in supply. How am I going to live long enough, waiting for a new liver?" He said, almost lashing out to the specialist.

"I am encouraging you, James. This is your only hope. I assure, you have nothing to lose, but everything to gain if a liver does become available," The specialist replied. James wanted to counter his words again, but the specialist seemed so sincere that it moved him so silence himself.

"With God, all things are possible," The specialist added, with a smile. James immediately raised an eyebrow at this additional remark from the specialist.

Before finding out about his bad liver and the desperate predicament he was currently in, any mention or reference about God would immediately raise a red flag for James. However, again, there was this sincerity in the specialist's words that seem to move James. Unbeknownst to him, his attitude and atheistic stand was slowly about to change.

Even the lady who worked in the office as a receptionist and was never intimidated or afraid to let her light shine around all the other workers was delightfully astounded to see the drastic change in James when he came into the office. One day when they were all alone, she was shocked when James asked her what it meant to be saved. To the best of her ability, she told him in simple layman's terms that it meant to believe in Jesus Christ as Lord and Savior and to accept Him into your heart. She was further astounded when he asked her more questions about God and Jesus Christ being His Only Begotten Son. The secretary was amazed at how God had prepared her to give him biblical answers to his questions that seemed to satisfy his desire to know about these spiritual things being that she was a serious student of the Bible who taught a young adults' class at her church. All of her years of studying and teaching the Scriptures were now paying off in the role that she had been chosen to play in James's life. Both the example that she had lived before her work peers and the man who was her employer were yielding fruit through her being able to give him answers of the hope that was in her.

As James's liver condition worsened and his body began to weaken, his hunger to know more about Jesus Christ and eternal life increased. The attitude of covetousness and materialism that once dominated his life was loosening its hold on him. He no longer ran his trucking company the way he once had. His staff and employees were baffled and glad at the change that had come over him. They all, without exception, preferred the changed man and boss that James was developing into. The receptionist that the Holy Spirit had used to instruct and enlighten him continued to make herself available to James and used every opportunity that presented itself to further feed his quest and hunger for spiritual truth.

The day came when James was under conviction and asked her this question during one of their talks:

"If I died right now," He asked her emphatically, "would I go to heaven or hell?"

She paused a while before she answered him and considered the consequences of not telling him the truth. Without any intimidation or reservation, she answered in a loving way.

"Sir," she said, "Before I answer your question, I would first like to ask you a question." He told her to ask the question and she inquired.

"Have you accepted Jesus Christ into your heart as your Lord and Savior?"

James hesitated for a moment and then responded, "No, I have not."

To his response, she said, "Then if you died right this moment, you would be lost and spend eternity in hell."

Expecting a somewhat negative remark to the truth that she had given him, she was both astounded and delighted when he said, "Well, is there any reason why I can't accept Christ right now?"

Overjoyed with tears in her eyes, she said, "No, there isn't."

She led him in the sinner's prayer and the man who had once been a hardcore atheist was born again into the family of God.

Almost miraculously a few weeks later, James received some very good news. He received a call from his doctor who was so full of joy when he told him that a liver had suddenly become available and that it was a perfect match for him. When James shared with him the good news of his conversion, they both rejoiced together over the phone at the timing and work of the Lord. There was no doubt in either of their minds that the Lord who had saved him had also made the liver available for him at that opportune time. The liver was immediately sent to the hospital where James was waiting to have the transplant operation performed. The procedure was a complete success without any complications or difficulties. Even the surgeon and everyone involved in the process were amazed at how well things went. James's body received his new liver without any rejection and after a few weeks in recovery he was back on his feet and running things again in his trucking company. However, James's total perspective and priorities in life had been altered now that he was a Christian. He became a bold witness for Jesus Christ and shared his testimony whenever and wherever he could.

James' conviction, conversion, and new liver that was a perfect match for his body had been answer to an organ donor's prayer—a man named Luke.

CHAPTER 7

A Politician's Last Hope

Daniel Dawkins had established himself as an up-and-coming politician over the last fifteen years. Starting out on the local level, he had won a seat on the County Council of the county government where he lived. He was the youngest person to ever be elected to the council, being only twenty-four when he took the oath of office.

Due to his natural good looks, charisma, and ambition, he was able to run for a higher political position in his district of the state where he lived. He made the risky decision to challenge a man who had been in politics for over thirty years. Most of those years had been spent in the position of being a state senator. The campaign between Daniel and his opponent had been one of the most fiercely fought with much mudslinging and name calling that the state had ever seen. At the end of the day, when all the votes had been counted, Daniel had won the election with the majority of the votes.

Nevertheless, the stress and strain of such a nasty and ugly campaign took a heavy toll on both men. His opponent in this political fight, being almost twice Daniel's age, had some serious underlying conditions. Not long after the intense and arduous season of campaigning, he succumbed to a stroke and died not many days afterwards. Daniel expected blatant backlash, but he received none. No one directly blamed Daniel, or pointed a finger at him, as being the cause of the former state senator's death. However, there was still much gossiping, whispering, secret talk and accusations in high places that laid the blame at his door. There was a lot of staring whenever Daniel would walk on the halls of the office building, but he was not bothered. Be it due to the fact that he was indeed innocent, or due to the fact that all he cared about was winning.

Dan, as he was called by those who knew him on a more intimate level, began to allow a bit of pride and conceit to form in his mind. After all, not only was he the youngest person to ever be elected to the County Council seat in the history of his county, but he had also both defeated a long-standing state senator and had the distinction of being one of the youngest senators in the state. Some who knew and dealt with him on a more personal and professional level began to detect the change in his attitude and demeanor. Where he had once been very accessible and empathetic to people, especially to the ones in his district, he was now hard to reach and started to avail himself primarily to people of prominence and position who could help to advance his political ambitions.

He had been bitten by the wasp of ambition and arrogance that completely altered his once pleasant and humble character. With his eyes set on becoming a United States congressman in a few years, State Senator Dan began to believe that he was politically unbeatable and unstoppable. The very people who had vested interest in him fed his ego with praises and compliments, due to the fact that he could do a lot of things for them from his position as a state senator. They also gave into his campaign coffers with large donations—both legally and under the table. But despite all of the drastic change that had swiftly taken place in Daniel Dawkins due to his meteoric rise, he still had a few good friends and supporters; those who still believed in him despite his departure from the path that he once walked upon.

Though Daniel had never claimed to be a Christian and had never accepted Jesus Christ into his heart as his Lord and Savior, he had come from a good Christian family and had been brought up attending church. Daniel had stopped attending church once he went to college and saw no practical need to attend with any degree of consistency or commitment. Nevertheless, he had retained some good Christian virtues and values from his upbringing. Sadly, even that was gradually slipping away too.

Janice was a close friend of Daniel who had been ever since they were in elementary school. At one point in time in high school when they were juniors, they considered themselves to be in a relationship for a few months, however, their relationship proved to be platonic and not romantic. Janice had managed to remain one of Daniel's closest and dearest friends who he would often confide in. Though they had gone in different professional directions, Daniel into politics and Janice into education as a teacher at a Christian school, they shared two things in common: they were both close friends and single. Janice had been a part of the core group who had spearheaded Daniel's campaign to be a state senator. When he would not listen to anyone else, he would listen to Janice.

Daniel, during a routine visit to his doctor, had received some disturbing news. For some inexplicable reason, his colon was beginning to dysfunction at a rapid pace. Further visits to a few intestinal specialists only confirmed that the young state senator was in a terminal state and only a new colon would save his life.

At the gloomy prognosis that Daniel had received from his doctors, all of his plans and ambitions dissolved into ashes. He was now preoccupied and possessed with the desire to live. In this depressed and desperate state, Daniel, who had once been a very proud and conceited man, was completely broken in spirit. He no longer seemed like the Daniel everyone knew. He was not humble Daniel or even prideful Daniel—he was just broken. It was like a cloud settled above his life. Daniel felt helpless, but no one is ever helpless.

It was exactly at this point that the Holy Spirit convicted him of the need to be saved. All of his life, especially as an adult, he had dismissed the issue of dying and where he would spend eternity. Having fluctuated between a belief in agnosticism and deism over the last few years of his life, mortality was setting in as something that would soon happen if he did not get a new colon in time from the donor's bank.

He decided to be sure about his eternal state so he called Janice, the one person he had much confidence in to be a true Christian.

"Is it too late for me to be saved?" He asked, once Janice accepted the call.

"What do you mean, Dan?" Janice asked, very confused with the sudden question from her friend.

"Is it too late for me to accept Him?" He asked again. Janice took a while before she realized what her friend was talking about.

"It's not too late, Dan. It's never too late," She replied, with so much sincerity that it brought her to tears. She was elated and full of joy.

"As long as you're sincere about accepting Him into your heart, Dan, then all will be well," Janice assured him. Daniel did not reply and let silence fill the minutes of their call.

"I can even do it for you right now, over the phone," Janice added.

"You can?" Daniel asked, bewildered.

"Yes, I can. He is everywhere and He knows your heart. He listens, Dan," She stated. This filled Daniel with so much emotion that he began to sob as he told Janice to pray for him. Janice, his long standing friend, led him to the Lord.

To his utter amazement, as he grew physically weaker and weaker, he received some good news from his doctor. They had found a colon in the nick of time for the young senator that would be a perfect match.

The transplant operation was a complete success and Daniel recovered quickly. He was able to resume his duty as a state senator with a new perspective and priorities in life. All thanks to the donor who made his life better now… a man named Luke.

CHAPTER 8

THE EX-CONVICT WHO BECAME A NEW CONVERT

Jacob stared on the road. It wasn't long since he'd seen the road that belonged to people who weren't convicted, but it had a different feel now. Today, he was released from prison. He looked back and couldn't believe what had happened for the past thirty years. Jacob felt a sense of joy, because he was finally out, but he was bitterer about it now. Especially now that there was something far greater that could imprison him, and even worse, kill him.

Before Jacob had been released from prison on an early release, he had had some serious problems with his kidneys. The condition had gotten worse and worse. He was granted an early release by some of the people who knew about his kidney problems and how the penal system often operated. His early release would help the government save from the high cost of taking care of him medically.

Jacob had always insisted that he was innocent of the charges that he was in prison for. He had spent over thirty years in the federal prison system during which time he had grown bitter and full of hostility toward people and authority. The anger and hatred that he held in his heart was especially there toward whites in authority. He blamed them for sentencing him for a crime he had not committed. Now that he was a free man, he felt more imprisoned than he had ever been. Jacob, who had been institutionalized by all the years he had spent in prison, did not know how he was going to function and how well he would fare on the outside. Compounding his considerations and challenges was the fact that his kidneys were malfunctioning and he had to go on a dialysis machine three times a week.

A few months before he left prison, when he first discovered that he had a kidney problem, he signed up to receive a kidney from a donor. This was done out of just having something to do in order to fill in the time and break the routine of prison life. In all actuality, he never believed that they would give a convict a new kidney to prolong his life. Though modern DNA detection had helped to get him released from prison after thirty years and proved his claim of innocence, Jacob felt that in the eyes of the world, he would always be considered as an ex-convict.

Once he had been released from prison, he discovered that most of his old buddies and friends that he once hung out with were either deceased, living in a nursing home, or had, for many years, moved to another state or city. Nevertheless, one of the men, who had been a close friend of his since their boyhood days, was still living in the area. He had accepted the call to ministry while Jacob was in prison and was now serving as a pastor in one of the churches in the area. As a matter of fact, his church had a very active prison ministry that would visit the prison where Jacob was serving his time. On one occasion, when his team visited the prison, he decided to accompany them. When he came up to speak to the inmates that had gathered for the service, as his eyes scanned the audience, he was surprised to see his old friend sitting and looking straight at him. Pastor Richards knew that Jacob was incarcerated somewhere in the state, however, he did not know that he was in an institution that was only about thirty miles from their hometown.

After the service was over, he was granted the opportunity by the officer in charge to talk with Jacob privately for a few minutes. Their talk was at first very formal and somewhat cold. Nevertheless, when Pastor Richards began to talk about their boyhood days and people who they both knew and were mutually friends with, Jacob's reservation and coldness thawed and he began to talk freely with his old buddy. He told him that he had only recently been transferred to the institution where they were. Furthermore, he shared that he was getting ready to be released after serving over thirty years in prison for a crime he had not committed. His old friend did the best he could to comfort and encourage him, especially about his bout with his kidney problems. As they departed, he assured him that he would be there for him and would continue to pray for his healing and well-being. He gave him a special invitation to come and visit him at both his home and church when he was released from prison.

Jacob had been out of prison for a few months and was having a difficult time adjusting and settling into his life as a civilian and free man. Having to be on the dialysis machine added to his challenge of adjusting. He had considered visiting his old friend's church a few times, but had reservations on how they would receive him. After all, he was an ex-convict who had spent over thirty years in prison. Sure, he was certain that his buddy would welcome him with open arms of compassion, but what about the members? This thought troubled him and was the primary reason why he never went–not only there, but to any church.

Pastor Richards, not wanting to be too aggressive and pushy, endeavored to be patient and prayerful about the matter. Then one day, he received a call from Jacob that he immediately detected was a distress call for help. Wasting no time at all, he dropped what he was doing and drove to his house. When Jacob met him at the door, he immediately discerned that he was in a very difficult place as his fallen and dejected countenance clearly expressed. Jacob's eyes were full of tears when he confessed to Pastor Richards that he was so discouraged, depressed, and confused that he felt like killing himself. In the dejected and discombobulated state that he was in, he felt that suicide was his only solution. Pastor Richards, being led by the Holy Spirit, prayed a special prayer of deliverance for his mind and the desire to take his own life.

Amazingly, he watched his old friend as his befuddled and downcast countenance changed. There was now a radiance upon his face, a look of hope and optimism. Pastor Richards sensed that the Lord was currently at work, through the Holy Spirit. They were convicting and preparing Jacob's once embittered and hardened heart to accept Jesus Christ into his life–to accept Jesus Christ into his life as his personal Lord and Savior.

"Are you willing now to accept Jesus Christ as your Lord and Savior, Jacob?" Pastor Richards, tearful at the sight of his old friend regaining radiance, asked. Jacob looked up to him, eyes filled with tears. But there was also something else that was filling in Jacob's eyes. It was hope.

"Yes, I am prepared to accept Him."

The man who had spent thirty-plus years in prison for a crime he always asserted that he did not commit was transformed by the power of God from being an ex-convict to being a new convert in Christ.

His old friend, Pastor Richards, took him under his wings and personal tutelage. Jacob grew in the grace of God and in the knowledge of his Lord and Savior Jesus Christ exponentially in the ensuing months. He joined Pastor Richards' church and became a faithful member.

Not long after his miraculous conversion, the Lord worked another miracle for him of a different nature. A kidney became available that was a perfect match for Jacob. The transplant operation was a complete success and Jacob's body accepted the new kidney without any complications. Both of these amazing and miraculous things happened in Jacob's life primarily because of a prayer made by a man named Luke.

CHAPTER 9

NEW HEART, NEW LIFE

Andrea had been born with Type 1 diabetes. It runs in the blood, she would always say to people when they see her inject insulin into her stomach or see her diabetes patch. The condition had always put Andrea and her family in and out of the hospital for many years now. She suffered multiple complications due to this illness and it even forced her family to go into debt. Her parents worked their back off, trying to pay her medical bills, treatment, and medicine, and also their living expenses and paying off their debts. Extreme fatigue and stress caused the very sudden death of her mother, which burdened her father more. Andrea made it a resolve upon herself to work on herself.

Andrea's parents were baptized Christians and so was she. However, they do not go to church every Sunday due to the fact that her parents had to get a double job just to pay for their expenses. Andrea, at a very young age, understood how hard her life was. She was an only child, but her parents' were working as if they had 10 children. Albeit not being able to attend to church, Andrea's mother would constantly tell her about the stories surrounding the church and Jesus Christ. She'd tell her how He was the One that would save the sinners from eternal doom and how God was all loving and kind. Growing up, Andrea believed this. It all somehow disappeared when her mother died when she was 15. At the age of 25 years old, she had finally finished college, despite the hindrances, and went on to work. She was finally supporting her own and her father, who never remarried. She was the breadwinner of their small family. Her father went back to going to church and even became a minister. Andrea, however, chose not to join her father because she had a different plan on her own.

Little by little, Andrea could feel that she was no longer feeling sick. She felt better, as she would say. So little by little, Andrea was letting herself loose. She would go on trips with friends, smoke, drink, and do stuff she wasn't able to do way back when she was 'sick'. Her father witnessed all these and was disappointed with how his daughter had seemingly neglected all the hard work he and his wife put on her just so she could live a healthy life.

One day, her father came back from church and called her for a talk.

"The church has this outreach program next week Sunday at the hospice nearby. We would be giving donations and supplies to the patients there. I thought, maybe you'd want to come to see the patients there," Her father said, calmly. Andrea scoffed.

"I dreaded my days living there. Why did you think it was a good idea to bring me back there?" She raised her voice, obviously offended by her father's invitation. Her father's head hung low, disappointed with what he just heard.

"I just thought you'd like to help, since you yourself understood how dreadful it was to live there. Maybe you can offer them words of encouragement, especially because you got to overcome it, by the grace of God," Her father replied. Once again, Andrea huffed in disbelief.

"I wished to die when I was there! I didn't want to live anymore! I prayed to your God to just kill me, but instead He took my mother! If there was anyone who ever helped me in overcoming what I felt way back then, it was me and me alone!" Andrea stormed out of the house and left.

It had been months since that happened and Andrea never talked to her father anymore. She never told anyone, not a single soul, about how she wanted to die when she was still sick and living in the hospice. Even if it was just for a year, it was dreadful for her. Her friends from back home would live a normal life. They get to go to school, they get to play, they get to eat anything they wanted, and they get to do anything they want. Living a different and sickly life was what made Andrea hate everything, but she just masked it off because she didn't want to discourage or hurt her parents. Now that she was old enough, she no longer cared.

Years passed and Andrea's father died. She was 28 years old at the time. She never got to say sorry to him—they never got to talk sincerely before he faced death. Andrea blamed herself for everything, but she was more mad at the One from up above.

"You said You would protect me and save me! Why have you left me all alone!" She would often scream in her cries. Andrea spent months wasting away, no longer caring about her job and about her health. Then, the day she dreaded the most happened.

"Have you been taking your prescriptions, Miss Andrea?"

"No."

"That explains. Along with the fatigue that caused you to faint, the pain you've been feeling these past few weeks was actually your pancreas. It has been performing in its lowest capacity and would soon no longer function."

"What can we do about it?"

"A transplant would be your best chance."

Her friend found her lying on the bathroom floor one day and immediately brought her to the hospital. She had actually been suppressing pain since the day her father had died because she thought it was just simply indigestion. However, as the doctor had explained to her, it was actually her pancreas failing already. Andrea fell into a deeper and darker pit. She was being swallowed by regret, hatred, sorrow, and pain. Her mind was clouded and she did not know what to do. But she wasn't alone. She had her friend, Meredith.

Meredith knew Andrea when they were children back then. They would often play together, despite Andrea's condition. When Andrea's condition worsened and she would frequent the hospital, Meredith no longer saw her. They reconnected when they began to work. Meredith became the friend Andrea never knew she needed. So when she was experiencing all this, Meredith was the only one who was beside her.

One day, Andrea woke up with Meredith praying next to her. Meredith was holding her hand as she was intently praying. Andrea could feel herself burst into tears, because it was probably the first time she had ever witnessed someone cry and pray for her. Meredith opened her eyes and saw how her friend was already in tears. They spent a good time crying together, while Meredith was mentioning the grace of the Holy Spirit being present between the both of them. There was a sudden shift in Andrea's heart–something she had never felt before–like a hug from her mother.

As soon as Andrea began to pray, Meredith asked her the biggest question.

"Are you ready now to accept Jesus Christ as your Lord and Savior?" Meredith asked, still teary eyed. Andrea sobbed hard and nodded multiple times.

"I am now ready, Meredith," She replied. She was led into the sinner's prayer and they filled the entire morning in prayer.

Almost immediately, Andrea received good news from her doctor. A pancreas had been available not long ago and she was the perfect match. They immediately sent her to the operation room and the transplant was conducted. Thanks to the grace of God, there were no complications and Andrea just needed for the wounds to heal so she could enjoy her life again as a Christian woman. Soon enough, the doctors told her the organ had been functioning perfectly and that she was good as new. With her new organ and new Christian heart, Andrea was eager to live a better life.

During Andrea's last night at the hospital, she decided to write a letter to the donor. She was intent into living a better life, so she decided it was good to start it by expressing her gratitude. Although she would never know on this side of eternity that it was a Christian brother named Luke whose prayer and pancreas had been the human factors that the Lord had used to save both her spiritual life as well as her natural life, it is certain in Heaven this amazing story would be revealed to her.

C H A P T E R 10

FINALE

"Is this everything?" The truck man asked.

Jane, Luke's wife, nodded. The last box was loaded to the truck and, soon after, the truck departed. Jane stood on their front porch for a good minute. She was trying to catch her breath, heaving a sigh. She was also trying to calm herself. It was the last of Luke's things that they decided to donate. It had already been a few weeks since his passing and they thought it would help them if they helped others and donated some stuff.

Jane went back in and went directly to their room. It had already been a lot of time since her husband had passed on, but she could still smell his scent all over the room. It almost brought her to tears, but she calmed herself down. She still had a lot of things to do. She still had to pick up the kids from school and make them dinner. Before that, she has to go to the grocery store to pick up a few things. Also, before she goes to the grocery store, she has to stop by the local bookstore to grab a few books.

It was pretty obvious that Jane was keeping herself occupied.

"Mom, can we please have pizza for dinner tonight, please?"

"Mom, my teacher said you have to sign these so she can make sure I am showing you my grades."

"Mom?"

Jane snapped out of it. The kids had been calling her and talking to her, but she was spaced out. She thought she was trying to drive carefully, but she was actually clouding her head with so many thoughts that she was no longer paying attention to neither–the kids or the road. Jane told the kids she was going to make dinner and although they had a few protests, she eventually got their 'approval'.

When they arrived home, Jane unloaded her groceries and the stuff she got as she went around the day. The kids were in their rooms and doing their homework or school projects. Jane was in the kitchen, preparing to cook for dinner. As Jane set out the ingredients, she suddenly felt extremely beaten. It was twilight already and the house was extremely silent. It was probably the first time Jane ever noticed how the house had fell silent after what happened to Luke. She stood there, over the counter, holding her weight so she wouldn't fall down.

The house was never silent when Luke was still there. The television would be turned on, some news channel would be heard, or maybe he would be on the living room with the kids, helping them with their homework. Sometimes, he would be right next to her, talking about how his day went while helping her prepare dinner. Luke made their home so warm that when he left, all Jane could see was coldness.

Jane carried on with what she was doing, almost barely. She proceeded into making the dinner, resolving unto herself on how to replace the warmth Luke has set upon their home. She called the children and, together, they had supper. Her eldest lead the saying of grace and they all had a very 'sumptuous' dinner.

"Mom, this is really good," Her youngest said, in a very soft tone. She just gave the small child a smile and held her face. The child was a splitting image of her father. It was just like hearing her husband compliment her all over again.

They finished and the kids were in their rooms again. Jane had done the dishes and she was off to bed as well. She cleaned up and sat for a while to read a book. Then, she prayed.

Ever since Luke's passing, Jane would pray that his husband's last prayer be fulfilled.

"God has a purpose with me and I honestly believe I won't die until I have fulfilled that purpose. Before I signed up to be an organ donor, I prayed that when I do die, He will let anyone who receives any of my blood or organs be a sinner who needed saving. And if it was His Will, to bring them to a saving knowledge of Jesus Christ."

That night, they prayed together and she heard him pray about it. Ever since then, she would always include that into her prayers.

"Lord, I honor you. I praise you, Almighty, and I follow You. Please hear me and husband's prayers. Let him be Your servant in this world, even though he had already joined You. Please let him be Your instrument in this world," She prayed.

The night had gone by and the next morning began. Jane woke up, still filled with coldness as she realized no one was beside her to greet her a good morning. Nonetheless, she went about her morning, because she had to. She made breakfast for the children, made their lunch, and then drove them to school. She went back home to clean up a little and went out again to visit the charity house she and Luke used to go to. This was also where she donated most of Luke's stuff. This charity desperately needed all kinds of help and by offering it so would help her sleep at night, knowing her husband's prayers are being answered with her help.

"Sister Jane, it is so nice to have you here. We are so thankful for your generosity," The sisters welcomed her. They had called her in for a cup of tea and then they enjoyed an early afternoon of helping the staff packing the donations for it to be sent to orphanages and camps dedicated for the homeless.

After helping there, she went home. For the first time, their mailbox had something in it. She got it and went inside their house. She made herself some tea before she sat on Luke's side of the couch and opened the envelope.

After reading the letter, Jane was moved to tears. It was a letter from a person named Andrea Hawkins, who had recently received Luke's organ. She was thanking him, telling how he became the answer to all her prayers. She was telling her about her story, how she became lost after battling her illness since her birth, and how when she started to believe in God again, he became the first person to grant her prayers. It was penned with so much gratitude that Jane began to feel warmth in her heart once again.

Luke's purpose had finally come to life. His life, as described once by his father, was like the life of Jesus Christ. He ceased to live, but in this way, he had served his purpose. His organs and his blood had gone to different people, all of which had seen the saving glory of the Lord. With that, they also saw a new life as they were given the grace to be saved physically and spiritually. Like Jesus Christ, he continued to live through the many lives of the people he had saved—the lives of the sinners who needed saving and needed the Word of God.

Luke's prayers were answered.